KU-760-387

A Globalist Manifesto for Public Policy

A Globalist Manifesto for Public Policy

The Tenth Annual IEA Hayek Memorial Lecture

CHARLES W. CALOMIRIS

Sponsored by

NOMURA

iea

The Institute of Economic Affairs

First published in Great Britain in 2002 by
The Institute of Economic Affairs
2 Lord North Street
Westminster
London SW1P 3LB
in association with Profile Books Ltd

Copyright © The Institute of Economic Affairs 2002

The moral right of the authors has been asserted.

All rights reserved. Without limiting the rights under copyright reserved above,
no part of this publication may be reproduced, stored or introduced into a
retrieval system, or transmitted, in any form or by any means (electronic,
mechanical, photocopying, recording or otherwise), without the prior written
permission of both the copyright owner and the publisher of this book.

A CIP catalogue record for this book is available from the British Library.

ISBN 0 255 36525 X

Many IEA publications are translated into languages other than English or are
reprinted. Permission to translate or to reprint should be sought from the
General Director at the address above.

Typeset in Stone by MacGuru
info@macguru.org.uk

Printed and bound in Great Britain by Hobbs the Printers

CONTENTS

THE AUTHOR

Charles W. Calomiris is a visiting scholar at the American Enterprise Institute, Paul M. Montrone Professor of Finance and Economics at Columbia University's Graduate School of Business, Professor of International and Public Affairs at Columbia's School of International and Public Affairs, and a research associate of the National Bureau of Economic Research. He has served on the International Financial Institution Advisory Commission, a congressional commission to advise the US government on the reform of the IMF, the World Bank, the regional development banks, and the WTO. Mr Calomiris's research spans several areas, including banking, corporate finance, financial history, and monetary economics. His recent publications include *US Bank Deregulation in Historical Perspective* (Cambridge University Press, 2000), *Emerging Financial Markets* (with David Beim, Irwin-McGraw-Hill, 2000), and 'Blueprints for a New Global Financial Architecture' in *International Financial Markets: The Challenge of Globalization* (Leonardo Auernheimer, ed., University of Chicago Press, 2000). Mr Calomiris also teaches a course for senior World Bank managers on bank regulation and exchange rate policy in developing economies, and a course on the same topic in the executive education programme at the IMF.

FOREWORD

The Tenth Annual IEA Hayek Memorial Lecture was an enlightening experience for us as students of economics and became a memorable occasion for us as the sponsor. In his lecture, Professor Charles Calomiris remembered the 1974 Nobel Prize-winner Friedrich von Hayek as an advocate of individual freedom as the best form of economic policy, and identified an outward economic orientation and a sound institutional framework as being the keys to economic prosperity. Professor Calomiris's analysis of the European, Chinese, US and Japanese experience was thorough and impeccable, and persuasively reinforced our belief in a free market and open society.

The best export from Great Britain to the rest of the world has been the concept of small government with a number of enabling tools, ranging from privatisation and deregulation to PFI and PPP. Japan has been one of many recipients of this wisdom; the current Japanese government is beginning a renewed offensive to reduce the weight of the public sector over what was a once healthy private-sector economy. Hayekian principles are too easily forgotten once people stop striving for them.

Nomura is grateful to Professor Calomiris for his outstanding lecture and to the IEA for giving us the opportunity to sponsor the event. Nomura's success relies in part on the relationships that we are able to develop with opinion-formers in the countries in which we operate, and how we interact with them to promote open and sometimes radical debate. We also rely on being able to work in a free and open economic environment, such as we experience here in Great Britain, which enables us to run our business efficiently to the benefit of all our stakeholders.

TAKUMI SHIBATA
President and CEO
Nomura International plc

As with all IEA publications, the views expressed in Professor Calomiris's paper are those of the author, not those of the Institute (which has no corporate view), its managing trustees, Academic Advisory Council or senior staff.

SUMMARY

- In the past two decades there have been many bold attempts
  at liberalisation. But there is now a backlash against
  'globalisation', which means it is premature for supporters of
  global economic freedom to celebrate.
- Nineteenth-century advocates of free international commerce
  realised that its benefits were not confined to static efficiency
  gains but include the way trade transforms society and
  reduces poverty. However, they understood the institutional
  barriers to economic development, as did Hayek:
  globalisation alone will not eliminate poverty or oppression.
- In the past, economic growth has been the result of an
  outward economic orientation combined with favourable
  domestic institutions (such as the rule of law and incentives
  to work and innovate). Cities and countries which discovered
  the right combination were the ones which thrived.
- Europe leapfrogged China because of its superior institutions:
  China had an inward orientation and interfered too much
  with private enterprise.
- In the postwar period, because of constraints on immigration
  into high-wage countries, trade and capital flows have been
  the dominant means through which globalisation has
  produced economic growth.
- Increasing income inequality among nations has come about

because participants in globalisation have enjoyed substantial gains, whereas the positions of other countries have deteriorated in absolute and relative terms.

- Competition in trade not only permits efficiency gains, it allows people and capital to move to countries with superior institutions. Moreover, the accompanying flow of ideas about politics and law makes repression difficult for oppressive regimes.
- Developing countries should open themselves to global competition in trade, to entry by foreign firms and to international capital flows. In today's environment, domestic protection merely produces rent-seeking, value-destroying firms.
- Reforming domestic institutions is also necessary. Particular requirements are predictable and impartial courts, legal protection of property and enforcement of contracts, absence of corruption and a commitment to avoiding inflationary budget deficits. Government should avoid protection of banks, which undermines market discipline.
- There is widespread support for globalisation among poor residents of developing countries. Proponents of globalisation need to find ways to make these voices of the poor heard among the din of demonstrations at international gatherings.

TABLES AND FIGURES

TABLES AND FIGURES

A GLOBALIST MANIFESTO FOR PUBLIC POLICY

The Tenth Annual IEA Hayek Memorial Lecture, delivered at One, Great George Street, London, SW1, 5 July 2001*

In 1960, in *The Constitution of Liberty*, Friedrich Hayek wrote that:

> Foreign policy today is largely a question of which political philosophy is to triumph over another; and our very survival may depend on our ability to rally a sufficiently strong part of the world behind a common ideal . . . the accomplishments of our civilisation have become the object of desire and envy of the rest of the world . . . a serious disappointment of their expectations would lead to grave international friction.

In that same book, Hayek also wrote that:

> What we must learn to understand is that human civilisation has a life of its own, that all our efforts to improve things must operate within a working whole which we cannot entirely control, and the operation of whose forces we can hope merely to facilitate and assist so far as we understand them. Our attitude ought to be similar to that of the physician toward a living organism: like him, we have to deal with a self-maintaining whole which is kept going by forces which we cannot replace and which we must therefore use in all we try to achieve.

*   I thank Allan Meltzer and Mary O'Grady for comments on a preliminary draft of this lecture.

In these two passages Hayek captured the essential policy challenge that faced the developed free world in its relations to the developing world *circa* 1960. At the height of the Cold War, promoting development to alleviate poverty abroad was not only the moral duty of the rich countries, or a means of expanding our economic opportunities, it was a matter of self-preservation in a world where communism and capitalism vied for global political influence.

But Hayek did not think it would be easy to make poor countries rich. Economies, he argued, are complex organisms; outside assistance and advice, like internal economic planning, are unlikely to be successful in turning a poor country into a rich one because the development of a successful economy is not the product of conscious intent or calculation, but rather of institutional adaptation over long periods of time. This was the basis for Hayek's view that individual freedom is the best economic plan.[1] Economic progress depends on humility about any one person's ability to produce economic progress by design, a philosophical humility that Hayek connected to the British tradition (and more distantly to the political philosophy of republican Rome), and which he distinguished from that of the French.

---

1   Hayek made this point repeatedly in *The Constitution of Liberty*: 'It might be said that civilisation begins when the individual in the pursuit of his ends can make use of more knowledge than he has himself acquired and when he can transcend the boundaries of his ignorance by profiting from knowledge he does not himself possess.' 'Not all the knowledge of the ever changing particular facts that man continually uses lends itself to organization or systematic exposition; much of it exists only dispersed among countless individuals.' 'The more men know, the smaller the share of all that knowledge becomes that any one mind can absorb. The more civilized we become, the more relatively ignorant must each individual be of the facts on which the working of his civilization depends.' 'And, once a more efficient tool is available, it will be used without our knowing why it is better, or even what the alternatives are.'

In the event, it was the demise of the Soviet Union rather than the success of rich countries in sharing their formula for prosperity which removed the threat to the security of the rich countries posed by global poverty. From a Hayekian perspective, of course, it is not surprising that the Soviet Union's grand experiment collapsed from technological stagnation and inefficiency, or that World Bank and other multilateral aid in pursuit of grand development projects to solve global poverty have failed so miserably to end poverty. The Soviets' failure was most obviously apparent not in growth rate or productivity statistics but in their inability to accomplish the ordinary small-scale achievements we take for granted, and on which grand success must be built. As David Landes writes in *The Wealth and Poverty of Nations*, 'The worse aspect of the [Soviet] system … was its indifference to, nay, its contempt for, good housekeeping and human decency. Prosperity forgone was bad enough. In a world that had once created and still preserved some beautiful things, the new system mass-produced ugliness: building and windows out of true; stained and pocked exteriors, raw cement block; equipment out of order, rusting machinery, abandoned metal corpses – in short, raging squalor.'[2]

One could say the same about the efforts of rich countries or their multilateral agencies to export economic development via ambitious grand schemes for agriculture and industry in poor countries.[3] As one angry citizen of debt-encumbered Mali

---

2   David Landes, *The Wealth and Poverty of Nations*, W.W. Norton, New York, 1999.

3   Landes also recounts the colossal failure of the British government's peanut-growing scheme in Tanganyika beginning in the mid-1940s. The planners boldly located the project on an empty site. It was empty because it had no water. Information on soil quality, rainfall, and their effects on yields was wanting. Costs of clearing the land were ten times original estimates, and the ground, once cleared, became extremely dry and hard. After years of stubborn, ill-fated efforts, the

commented: 'The West told us to build power stations, bridges, factories, steel mills, phosphate mines. We built them because you said so, and the way you told us. But now they don't work, you tell us we must pay for them with our money. That is not fair. You told us to build them, you should pay for them. We didn't want them.'[4] The man has a point.

When the plans of market participants fail, they disappear. But the bold economic plans of governments can persist for decades. Even worse, they crowd out private initiatives that would mitigate the social costs of government failure. Government enterprises are financed by taxes and by government control of the banking system, which ensure a ready supply of funds to finance state-mandated investments. State-controlled banks give free rein to value destruction by state-owned production plants, and make it virtually impossible for private entrepreneurs to finance any alternatives to the wasteful state-controlled system.

The collapse of the Soviet façade of economic progress, and the failures of dirigiste economic development policy in the 1950s, 1960s and 1970s, eventually pointed many developing countries in a new direction. The 1980s and 1990s saw many bold attempts to liberalise. One might even say that the past two decades have seen a revolution in economic policy in many of the world's poor

---

project was abandoned, with the equipment left to rot (Chapter 28).

Landes's favourite example of industrial overreach is the Algerian débâcle of the 1980s. In the 1970s, socialist Algeria's minister of industry proclaimed it 'Africa's first, and the world's second, Japan'. Algeria embarked on an economic plan that emphasised state-designed heavy industry. The product of this industry found no external market, and was virtually unusable even domestically. The effort was abandoned and the equipment left to waste or cannibalised. The manufacturing sector collapsed. This was the rule rather than the exception.

4   Landes, op. cit., Chapter 28.

economies. So-called 'emerging market economies' have abandoned state control over substantial portions of their economies, liberalised their trade policies, deregulated and privatised their domestic financial systems, permitted entry by foreign-owned firms on an equal footing with domestic firms, and come to rely increasingly on vast new private sources of international capital. Communications links across countries have substantially reduced effective economic distance. Individuals can trade securities 24 hours a day by moving around the globe from one market to another. American consumers routinely receive customer assistance via telephone from Asian residents who feign American accents and use American pseudonyms. Not since World War I has the flow of capital and trade been so great, and the flows of private debt and equity capital to developing countries are unprecedented. From the perspectives of the rate of foreign entry by firms, the distances spanned in daily business communication, and the international diversification of individuals' portfolios, the world has never been so 'global'.

This should be a time of great celebration for advocates of global economic freedom. It is not. Instead, we are seeing the beginning of a backlash against globalisation. To some extent this is just the predictable reaction of sore losers – those in previously protected sectors who now find it harder to compete. That is nothing new or unexpected (earlier, successful waves of globalisation also saw similar protests). And there is also a predictable element of this backlash originating within the leftist intelligentsia and the labour unions of the developed countries – what David Henderson has so aptly labelled the 'new millennium collectivism'.[5] But there

---

5   David Henderson, *Anti-Liberalism 2000: The Rise of the New Millennium Collectivism*, Wincott Lecture, Occasional Paper 115, Institute of Economic Affairs, 2001.

is more to the current backlash than those influences. Overall economic progress has been slow in some developing economies and volatile in others, leading some critics to argue that globalisation and liberalisation are not helping the poor to become rich. Is globalisation failing to deliver? Have economists sold the world a false promise?

In this paper I will review the case for globalisation from the perspective of the history of economic development, consider whether it has in fact been a disappointment, and suggest ways to magnify the rewards of globalisation. The result is what I have labelled a 'globalist manifesto' – an attempt to take stock of history and derive useful, empirically based policy prescriptions. I will show that there have been demonstrable gains to the poor from global flows of commodities, capital and labour, in the distant and the recent past. And an outward orientation often has encouraged institutional and political changes that expand the frontiers of economic achievement and individual rights, which, in turn, magnify the rewards of free trade and capital flows.

Globalisation in theory

The gains from globalisation that I will review have been noted throughout the ages by advocates of economic freedom. In *The Wealth of Nations*, Adam Smith argued that by expanding the extent of the market a domestic producer could reap economies of scale in production and increase national wealth. But that was not his only, or even his main, argument for free trade. Smith, echoing David Hume, argued that expanded commerce produced good government, and thus reduced the propensity for war, enhanced individual liberty and security, and promoted equality by lessening the 'servile dependency' of individuals on their superiors. The effect of increased commerce on individual freedom, Smith said, was relatively neglected by scholars – he called it the 'least observed advantage of commerce' and 'by far the most important of all [its] effects'.

David Ricardo refined the economic theory of the gains from trade, emphasising that commerce encouraged specialisation within countries and enriched consumers by allowing countries to produce in the areas of their greatest comparative advantage.

John Stuart Mill echoed these Ricardian and Smithian arguments, and also emphasised what he called additional 'indirect' gains from openness. Here he mainly had in mind the flow of information that accompanied trade. He noted that commerce enhanced the transfer of technology and the cultivation of refined tastes. But he went farther; like Smith, Mill saw the gains from economic linkages across countries in broader terms. In *Principles of Political Economy*, Mill wrote that:

> ... the economical advantages of commerce are surpassed in importance by those of its effects, which are intellectual and moral. It is hardly possible to overrate the value, in the present low state of human improvement, of placing human beings in contact with persons dissimilar to themselves, and with modes of thought and action unlike those with which they are familiar. Commerce is now, what war once was, the principal source of this contact ... There is no nation which does not need to borrow from others, not merely particular arts or practices, but essential points of character in which its own type is inferior.

And Mill, like Smith before him, saw commerce as a means to avert war: '... it may be said without exaggeration that the great extent and rapid increase in international trade, in being the principal guarantee of the peace of the world, is the great permanent security for the uninterrupted progress of the ideas, the institutions, and the character of the human race.'

Clearly, the great advocates of free international commerce did not conceive of its long-term gains merely or primarily as the static efficiency gains of the Ricardian model, but rather as improvements in the ideas and opportunities available to ordinary citizens, and as a spur to improvement of education, moral sentiments and individual character. It follows that the greatest transformation in living standards from free international commerce in a free society should accrue to the poorest within poor countries, since they stand to gain the most from expanded opportunity. Thus the argument for free trade, understood properly, is not just based on efficiency gains, but also on the way trade transforms society and thereby reduces poverty.

Two caveats about the advantages of globalisation were recognised by its historical advocates. First, short-term gains could be distributed differently from long-term gains, as it takes a long time for dynamic institutional and cultural effects to take hold. The richest residents in developing countries might benefit the most from liberalisation in the short run, but over longer stretches of time the poor will catch up. That phenomenon, as an empirical matter, is closely related to what is sometimes called the Kuznets curve (the tendency for spurts of economic progress to first widen, and later narrow, the wealth distribution).

Second, despite the tendency of classical economists to stress causal links from free trade to increased average wealth, poverty alleviation, peace, and individual freedom, it would be a caricature to view those philosophers as simple-minded economic determinists. For example, in his discussion of Chinese economic progress, Adam

Smith does not suggest that the removal of barriers to trade alone would transform eighteenth-century China into the political and economic equal of Great Britain. Instead he remarks that China, for perhaps more than five hundred years, had remained stagnant, having 'acquired that full complement of riches *which the nature of its laws and institutions permits it to acquire*' (emphasis added).

Mill was even clearer about the institutional and cultural barriers to economic improvement. He traced differences in the productive potential of countries not only to differences in technology or human capital, but also to the 'moral qualities of the labourers' and to differences in the 'energy of labour', which he in turn linked to geographical and climatic origins (a point of view that Jared Diamond has given new life in his recent treatise, *Guns, Germs and Steel*, W.W. Norton, New York, 1999). Mill also emphasised what he called 'security', by which he meant

> the completeness of the protection which the society afford to its members. This consists of protection *by* the government, and protection *against* the government. The latter is the more important. When a person known to possess anything worth taking away can expect nothing but to have it torn from him, with every circumstance of tyrannical violence, by the agents of a rapacious government, it is not likely that many will exert themselves to produce much more than necessities.

More recently, in *The Constitution of Liberty*, Friedrich Hayek addressed in detail the ways in which the infrastructure of laws, institutions and cultural values affects the ability of the economic system to deliver efficiency and growth. Hayek called these the 'tools' of successful adaptation. He saw them as the product of centuries of unconscious learning, derived from the culture and legal tradition especially of England. 'They consist in a large measure of forms of conduct which [man] habitually follows without knowing why; they consist of what we call "traditions" and "institutions", which [are used] because they are available ... as a product of cumulative growth without ever having been designed by any one mind.' While Hayek recognised that countries could usefully learn from one another's ethical precepts and institutional history, he believed that meaningful and lasting economic progress must be grounded in the deeply rooted evolution of institutions and individual attitudes. The process of transferring institutions and attitudes across countries is much slower and more subject to failure than the process of transferring technical knowledge.

It is fair to say, then, that although the most prominent proponents of free trade have been optimistic about its tendency to promote wealth, peace, individual opportunity and individual freedom, they did not claim that globalisation, by itself, would necessarily eliminate poverty or oppression in most or all poor countries. It is quite appropriate for eminent historians like David Landes to upbraid today's economists for their ignorance about the cultural and institutional constraints that have limited economic development in many countries over the past millennium. But the most famous advocates of globalisation shared Landes's appreciation for the many institutional and cultural preconditions for successful economic development.

In summary, although economic philosophers through the ages have always known that global linkages are not a panacea for poverty, disease, war and oppression (nothing ever is), they have shared an appreciation of the powerful arguments and evidence in favour of globalisation, especially from the perspective of the world's poorest countries.

Globalisation in history: a preview

I will address two key questions in my review of history. First, does an outward economic orientation produce the gains imagined in theory? Is it true that global economic liberalisation promotes efficiency, growth and institutional progress, and ultimately raises the condition of the poor the most? Second, which features of the domestic economic environment are most important for either magnifying or limiting the potential gains from globalisation?

When reviewing a thousand years of world economic history, it helps to have a central theme that ties the various epochs and events together. For Marx that theme was the inexorable march towards communism via dialectical materialism, recurring class struggles that pushed history forward. I will stress a different theme, the role of outward economic orientation in improving the lot of ordinary people, especially poor people. There are, of course, counter-examples. The trick to learning something useful from the history of the last millennium is in identifying the patterns that distinguish success from failure, and thereby constructing policy approaches that favour good outcomes. A second important theme of my historical review is that the gains to poor countries produced by an outward economic orientation are greatest when domestic legal, financial and political institutions are conducive to individual freedom, rule of law and competition. This implies that the gains enjoyed by a country from participating in the global economy will typically increase over time. An outward orientation encourages institutional, political and even cultural changes that expand the frontiers of economic achievement and individual rights.

The mechanisms through which global linkages have led to economic improvement can be divided usefully into four categories: (1) international competition in commodity markets promoted efficiency gains in production that raised wages and profits. Efficiency gains included static Ricardian gains from trade, and dynamic improvements from the transfer of technology, as producers struggled to remain internationally competitive; (2) freedom- and wealth-enhancing improvements in institutional infrastructure reflected broader exchanges of ideas about science, philosophy, law, religion and politics, especially once low-cost paper production and printing made rapid and widespread sharing of information possible; (3) freedom of emigration and capital flows across locations raised wages (particularly for the poorest segment of society) and raised returns to capital; (4) improvements in the political and economic freedom and power enjoyed by ordinary people resulted from the willingness of rulers to grant new rights to their subjects, which reflected international political and economic competition among those rulers.

Of the four mechanisms, the last is seldom emphasised by economists, but I think it may be the most important of all. As Douglass North and Robert Thomas, Eric Jones, David Landes, Angus Maddison and Joel Mokyr all have stressed in their landmark works exploring the history of European economic exceptionalism, political competition within Europe fuelled the search by the powerful for ways to improve economic performance and expand the geographical range of their influence.[6] Outward economic orientation was embodied in exploration, conquest and

---

6   Douglass C. North and Robert P. Thomas, *The Rise of the Western World*, Cambridge University Press, Cambridge, 1973; Eric L. Jones, *The European Miracle*, 2nd ed., Cambridge University Press, Cambridge, 1988; David S. Landes, *The Wealth and Poverty of Nations*, W.W. Norton, New York, 1999; Angus Maddison, *The World Economy: A Millennial Perspective*, OECD, Paris, 2001; and Joel Mokyr, *The Lever of Riches*, Oxford University Press, Oxford, 1990.

trade, entrepreneurship, emigration and foreign investment, and an interest in technological dynamism. Competition among sovereigns or nobles also had immediate and direct effects on improvements in domestic legal and political institutions, which secured greater freedom and power for the lower classes. *Global competition created strong incentives for domestic rulers to share power.*

The four channels through which outward orientation promoted progress (trade and technology flows, broader information flows, emigration and capital flows, and expanded personal freedom) all reinforced one another. The cities or nations that were best at harnessing these sources of gain dominated their eras economically and politically, and their successes encouraged imitation by competitors. Initially, that competition occurred largely within Europe, but eventually it spread outside Europe, as well, as other nations came to compete with, and learn from, the European states.

A brief economic history of the last millennium

The history of human progress over the past millennium is typically divided into sub-periods that correspond to important structural changes in politics and economics: (1) the early period, which saw important advances in technology in agriculture, water power, timepieces, paper production and countless other mundane but important innovations (such as spectacles), and which established a commercial network within Europe and one linking Europe to Asia via the Mediterranean (roughly 1000–1400); (2) the age of exploration, conquest and European nation and empire building, with its important technological advances in navigation, weapons and printing (roughly 1400–1700); (3) the era of proto-industrialisation and the first industrial revolution, involving especially new ways of manufacturing textiles and iron (1700–1850); (4) the era of the second industrial revolution, involving the widespread application of steam power, large-scale manufacturing and new products, especially in the areas of steel, chemicals and electricity (1850–1913); (5) the troubled period of worldwide war, depression and more war from 1913 to 1947; (6) the postwar period.

Over time, corresponding to improvements in technology and trade, the world has seen dramatic gains in income, but those gains have been concentrated in a few countries. Table 1 reviews some simple statistics that capture broad trends and regional differences in the growth of per capita income (in 1990 dollars) over the last millennium, taken from Angus Maddison's *The World Economy: A Millennial Perspective*. From the perspective of these statistics, the fundamental three questions of interest to world economic historians are: (1) Why did Europe get so rich relative to other regions – a pattern that began in the Middle Ages, and accelerated after 1500? (2) Why did North America (and later North America, Australia and New Zealand) grow faster than South America in the eighteenth, nineteenth and twentieth centuries? (3) Why was Japan so exceptional in its growth relative to other non-European countries in the nineteenth and twentieth centuries (a pattern that was repeated much later by its erstwhile colonies, Korea and Taiwan)?

Maddison argues that *circa* AD 400 average per capita income was roughly equal to its minimal subsistence level throughout the world. By 1500 (before the great opening of the sixteenth century), western Europe had nearly doubled its per capita income, while other regions remained stagnant. Maddison estimates that western Europe's per capita income surpassed China's at around AD

Table 1 **GDP per capita ($ 1990)**

	1000	1500	1700	1820	1870	1913	1973	1998
United Kingdom	400	714	1,250	1,707	3,191	4,921	12,022	18,714
Western Europe	400	774	1,024	1,232	1,974	3,473	11,534	17,921
Eastern Europe	400	462	566	636	871	1,527	4,985	5,461
Former USSR	400	500	611	689	943	1,488	6,058	3,893
US+CA+AUS+NZ	400	400	473	1,201	2,431	5,257	16,172	26,416
Latin America	400	416	529	665	698	1,511	4,531	5,795
Japan	425	500	570	669	737	1,387	11,439	20,413
Rest of Asia	450	572	571	575	543	640	1,231	2,936
Africa	416	400	400	418	444	585	1,365	1,368
World	435	565	615	667	867	1,510	4,104	5,709

Source: Angus Maddison, *The World Economy: A Millennial Perspective*, OECD, 2001.

1300; by 1820 western Europe enjoyed twice the per capita income of China; and by 1870 nearly four times China's per capita income. As late as 1950, Africa was struggling to maintain levels of per capita income that Europe had surpassed in 1600. China was even more retarded in its progress; as late as 1973, Chinese per capita income was lower than that of Europe in 1600. In contrast, Japan surpassed Africa and the rest of Asia in the eighteenth century, and by 1913 Japan enjoyed per capita income comparable to many southern and eastern European economies.

The areas of new European settlement also saw dramatic differences in growth over time. The areas of new British settlement – the US, Canada, New Zealand and Australia (which Maddison refers to as the 'Western offshoots') – caught up with western European per capita income by about 1820 and then forged ahead of Europe. Latin America followed a different and more backward path, roughly coincident with that of Japan until the postwar era, after which it fell farther behind the 'high wealth club' of western Europe, the Western offshoots and Japan.

There is broad agreement among economic historians about the reasons behind these differences in per capita income growth across regions. In essence, growth was the predictable consequence of a combination of outward economic orientation with favourable domestic institutions (especially, the presence of the rule of law and other preconditions favourable to individual freedom and to individuals' incentives to work and innovate). The first cities, and later countries, to hit upon the right combination of individual incentives and access to markets thrived and were imitated.

Political fragmentation in medieval Europe decentralised authority and spurred continuing competition among rulers. European civilisation was unique in this respect – a fact that reflected climatic and geographic factors peculiar to Europe. That political fragmentation and competition, combined with the cultural inheritance of Roman, Christian and Germanic traditions, fostered the concepts of private property and individual rights.

It is worth emphasising that early European growth was especially beneficial to the poor. The end of serfdom in western Europe was the result of increasing competition among rulers, which often took the form of constructing towns and cities – an outward-looking entrepreneurial act by medieval lords in search of new market opportunities. Towns had to be populated to be successful, so cities became 'gateways to freedom' for serfs, some of whom were explicitly granted freedom by entrepreneurial city-building lords. Competing medieval lords were also active proponents of technological progress, which substantially improved European agricultural productivity. As trade and freedom flourished, so did technological progress, and new ways of organising life emerged – working for wages, living in towns and cities.

A lord in search of new wealth and power was encouraged to co-operate rather than coerce as a means of expanding his power. That pattern would reappear. Exploration and conquest, and technological improvements in navigation and weaponry, owed their origins to political competition. But private gains were an inevitable result. Those private gains took the form of trading or mineral rights granted to merchants or explorers, and land grants to colonists in America during the seventeenth and eighteenth centuries.

Each epoch of global competition had clear winners and losers. Venice's reign gave way to those of intrepid Portugal and Spain in the fifteenth and sixteenth centuries, and they in turn were displaced by the superior cultivation-based empire-building strategies and entrepreneurship of the Dutch and British in the seventeenth and eighteenth centuries. European trade, technology, wealth and manufacturing flourished withal. And alongside these grew an international network of great minds and entrepreneurs devoted to applied scientific inquiry. Thus was the groundwork laid for the industrial revolution.

In Europe, then, power-hungry, greedy despots made beneficent rulers and patrons of technology. Trade routes expanded, technology was rapidly disseminated, and progress was cumulative (each improvement built on its predecessor).

Not so in Asia. Despite China's superior technological capabilities – in particular, its knowledge of printing, iron-making, paper production, water power, gunpowder, navigation, shipbuilding and water-powered textile spinning hundreds of years prior to their emergence in Europe – China failed to take advantage of that knowledge, and tended to forget or purposely ignore useful information. Eric Jones argues that Europe leapfrogged China because of shortcomings in the set of rules and institutions governing participation in the Chinese economy, and because of the political structure of China, which prevented an adaptation towards a more efficient set of rules. David Landes similarly writes that:

> The Chinese state was always interfering with private enterprise – taking over lucrative activities, prohibiting others, manipulating prices, exacting bribes, curtailing private enrichment. A favourite target was maritime trade, which the Heavenly Kingdom saw as a diversion from imperial concerns, as a divisive force and source of income inequality, worse yet, as an invitation to exit.

Ironically, the Chinese empire's political stability contributed to its inward orientation and retarded growth. As Eric Jones writes, 'Individual merchants might bribe their way to influence, but emperors never needed to rely on them as impecunious European kings did, and they did not gain influence as a class.' Emperors faced little external threat. Indeed, they perceived the main threat to their power as coming from a growing domestic merchant class, which might increase its wealth and power if permitted to do so via free trade and expanded property rights. The Ming emperors (1368–1844), in particular, felt threatened by the expansion of markets and went out of their way to put an end to industrialisation, international trade and foreign exploration. These emperors favoured a shift back to agriculture, demolished the Chinese astronomical clock constructed in 1090, allowed their navy to decay from disuse, and banned foreign trade. By the mid-sixteenth century the centuries-old Chinese art of shipbuilding was forgotten.

Scholars have long puzzled over the stubbornness of the Chinese failure to adopt new practices, even in the eighteenth and nineteenth centuries, even in the most obvious area of munitions.

That failure reflected an imperial strategy that feared local empowerment (guns could be turned on the ruler), and was designed institutionally to resist change or even the suggestion that improvement might be warranted. From the emperor's perspective, that strategy was quite successful. The emperor's goal was to maintain stasis (which served his lifestyle quite well). Consider, in contrast, the unprofitable British experience in America: decades of investment in exploration, settlement and military protection, accompanied by power-sharing in the form of grants of land and a large degree of political self-determination to colonists, all of which encouraged greater demands for independence, and ultimately resulted in the loss of resources and the creation of a powerful rival.

It is ironic that, despite the institutional shortcomings of the Chinese empire historically, in many respects Chinese culture seems to be especially conducive to capitalist development, but the constraints of its political system were overwhelming. Not only can one point to the inventiveness of ancient Chinese scientists as evidence of the potential for development in China; Chinese emigrants have been among the most successful entrepreneurs in Asia and elsewhere. As Landes notes:

> [in] Indonesia, where the Chinese form 4 percent of the population, they controlled in the early 1900s seventeen of the twenty-five largest business groups. In Thailand [today] (10 percent Chinese), they number more than 90 percent of the richest families and own the same proportion of commercial and manufacturing assets.[7]

---

7   One can make a similar point by comparing the relative economic performance of North and South Korea, or East and West Germany: all these comparisons demonstrate that, holding 'culture' constant, institutions matter, specifically institutions that either encourage or discourage individual initiative.

China's approach was the rule rather than the exception. Similar stories of persistent lack of technological progress or commercial energy can be related for Moghul India, Arabia and the Ottoman Empire. None of these institutional environments encouraged or rewarded entrepreneurial or inventive efforts. Individuals enjoyed few rights and suffered many duties. Taxation of the peasantry in the Moghul empire, for example, was particularly onerous, and local rulers had little stake in local success. As in China, Moghul aristocratic title to land was not hereditary.[8]

Political competition between these empires and the West widened the chasm between them. Unlike outward-oriented European states, which responded to competition by expanding the range of internal power-sharing, the Eastern empires responded to losses of territory or trading routes by squeezing their own subjects all the more. Thus stagnant growth became persistent decline. That decline did not reflect a lack of interest in wealth, *per se*,

---

8   Although it is not important for our present purposes, I note in passing that economic historians are also rediscovering the importance of geography in explaining the locational origins of economic success. Europe and Asia were favourable locations for building early agricultural economies – on which the development of towns and cities depends – owing to their temperate climates. European temperatures, in particular, permit year-round harvesting of crops – a consequence of the Gulf Stream. That harvesting pattern, along with ample water and land for pasture and a favourable climate for raising livestock, encouraged European use of horses and cattle, which had multiple advantages for agricultural productivity and improved the European diet, which likely made Europeans more fit and productive. Also, Europe's generous and even rainfall patterns and divided landscape encouraged greater political decentralisation than in Asia, where centralised riverine civilisations predominated. Some scholars believe these factors may explain early differences between Europe and Asia in the relative development of the concept of individual freedom. Even today, many tropical areas still suffer from extreme disadvantages related to disease which some believe have important ramifications for labour productivity and economic incentives.

but rather an unwillingness to allow individual freedom and market incentives to direct economic progress.

What was the common source of European exceptionalism in its attitudes towards individual freedom and private property rights, and why did Britain lead the way for Europe? As I have already suggested, political fragmentation and competition were key ingredients. The Judeo-Christian tradition, no doubt, contributed to an emphasis on individual freedom through its emphasis on individual worth and choice, as well.

There are a multitude of contributing factors that explain why Great Britain was poised to overtake the rest of Europe both as an empire builder and as an industrial dynamo. But the many causes that have been put forward for British dominance in the eighteenth and nineteenth centuries (the pre-existing network of local markets and developed transportation system, the presence of a skilled labour force, high literacy and the prevalence of applied scientific knowledge, the relative weakness of protective guilds blocking technological progress) all reflected a different role of the individual in English society which can be traced back to at least the thirteenth century. That role was visible in the relatively early emancipation of English serfs and the reliance on geographically and socially mobile wage labour, in the greater equality of women in English society and the relative absence of arranged marriage, in uniquely early attitudes about the relative importance of individual as opposed to communal decision-making. Alan Macfarlane, in *The Origins of English Individualism*, emphasised these early English traits and linked them to a unique early reliance on primogeniture in England, which he argues fostered individualism and the development of markets.

The emphasis on individual rights in England was codified

through the Magna Carta (1215) and its extension to commoners, in the development of the basic rule of law under common-law principles that ensured predictability and equality of enforcement by the courts, and in the willingness of British commoners to enlarge and preserve their rights (as during the English Peasants' Revolt of 1381, and the Glorious Revolution of 1688). Britain was the land where individual rights, private property and market relations thrived, and for that reason its citizens faced strong incentives to create wealth. England also attracted educated and innovative discontents from elsewhere in Europe.

As the dissemination of industrialisation and growth in per capita income in western Europe and the Western offshoot countries shows, it was possible to imitate first British, and later western European, success. But not all countries were equally able to do so. Scandinavia and the Netherlands, which most resembled Britain in their institutional and cultural milieu, were successful followers, and competitive pressures eventually encouraged favourable adaptations in France, Germany and elsewhere. New areas of British settlement inherited Britain's institutional arrangements – indeed, as Edmund Burke noted in his defence of the colonies' rebellion against Britain, America contained many of the most fervent adherents to the constitutional principles of 1688 (perhaps more than the mother country), and these principles of law and individual right were at the centre of the American Revolution. The American systems of manufacturing and land ownership that paved the way to American economic supremacy by the end of the nineteenth century were built on the foundation of British law and political institutions.

Japan is the most interesting case of successful catching up. It is the important exception to the pattern of slow Asian development. Its exceptional growth resulted from its effort to imitate Western economic success. Japan did so consciously, systematically, and at a deep institutional level. It retained, of course, distinct cultural elements, but it succeeded in large part because it was determined to transform itself from top to bottom to make capitalism work.

From its first contact with the West, the Japanese attitude was unique. Japanese rulers were impressed by Western achievements, and sought trade, information and ways to improve their lot. Ambition was an important pre-existing characteristic, and may have reflected Japan's political fragmentation (Japan consisted of separately controlled regional fiefdoms, nominally subservient to the emperor – in some ways reminiscent of medieval Europe and quite different from China). Japan suspended its initial trade connections with Europe as part of a purge of Christianity in the late seventeenth century. The country was isolated from the West for two centuries, during which frequent and bloody peasant uprisings transformed the relations between lords and peasants. This was Japan's version of medieval serf emancipation. The country's internal markets expanded alongside improvements in roads and technological progress in agriculture, resulting in substantial increases in land under cultivation and agricultural productivity (which is estimated to have risen by 30–50 per cent from 1600 to 1867). The manufacturing of cotton spread during this period as well, and the concentration of population in cities and towns followed. Japan was undergoing an economic transformation remarkably similar to that which England had undergone centuries before.

The commitment to modernisation in Japan, and the establishment of close connections with the West, came in the mid-nineteenth century, when the country abolished its feudal institutions, opened its trade, and began to establish a full complement of Western institutions. Universal education was mandatory, including primary education for girls. Japanese industrial progress was rapid, beginning with water power and cotton textiles manufacturing, and rapidly progressing to the production of second-industrial-revolution products, including machinery. And, of course, that was just the beginning.

During the pre-World War I era, Japan's growth was exceptional. As the data on per capita income show, other countries outside western Europe or areas of British colonisation failed to replicate successful industrialisation and wealth creation.

The relatively slow growth of Latin America in the nineteenth and twentieth centuries has been the subject of lengthy debate. Although undoubtedly the United States enjoyed some natural advantages (for example, the convenient placement of coal and iron resources, and the favourable climate for agriculture), and also was populated by residents of the home country in a more favourable way than in Latin America (that is, by permanent settlers in search of freedom and opportunity who initially became small landowners), such factors do not fully explain the difference. Spanish taxation was higher than British, and its restrictions on trade more severe.

Cultural and legal traditions mattered too, and still do. Latin American development lacked religious diversity and tolerance, and was founded on Napoleonic legal tradition, in which basic rights of creditors and minority stockholders are poorly protected. Much recent research on postwar economic performance around the world still finds that the legal traditions of developing countries (British, French or German) have enormous explanatory power for financial and economic development, after allowing for other influences.

In other areas – notably India – some have blamed imperialism for slow growth. In *The Tentacles of Progress* (Oxford University Press, Oxford, 1988), Daniel Headrick argues that the failure to establish educational systems that transferred practical knowledge, and the importation of machinery, meant that India's textile industry could not develop the human capital and experience with tinkering that are necessary to be competitive and innovative. No doubt. But does that argument explain why Japan *was* able to compete and grow, or why India failed to grow more rapidly in the late twentieth century?

Of course, the range of views on what is essential for successful development is enormous. Some scholars focus on the absence of skilled labour, others on missing scientific and technical knowledge, and still others on the repression of financial institutions. All of these arguments have merit, but to a great extent these are symptoms of deeper problems that both give rise to these failings and prevent people from overcoming them.

Another perspective on the importance of institutions comes from microeconomic studies of nineteenth- and twentieth-century underdevelopment. Gregory Clark has shown that poor economic growth coincided with low productivity at the level of the individual firm. Clark allows for differences in technology, and access to capital and labour, and finds that underdevelopment is traceable in the main not to differences in these factors between developed and developing economies, but rather to the inefficiency with which technologies and factors were employed in developing countries. He finds that moving the same factory, with the same management and skilled labour team, to a developing country

Table 2 **Income per capita and total factor productivity,
selected countries**

	Relative GDP per capita in 1910	Relative GDP per capita in 1990	Efficiency (TFP) in 1910	Efficiency (TFP) in 1990
USA	9.4	14.3	3.9	4.4
Great Britain	8.0	10.5	4.4	3.8
Argentina	7.6	3.7	4.0	2.3
Japan	3.5	11.3	2.8	2.7
Thailand	1.6	2.8	1.3	1.5
Korea	1.5	5.3	1.5	2.4
Indonesia	1.3	1.6	1.2	na
Zimbabwe	na	0.9	na	0.6
India	1.0	1.0	na	na

Source: Gregory Clark and Robert Feenstra, 'Technology in the Great Divergence',
Working Paper, UC-Davis, 2001, Table 1.

results in a substantial decline in the physical productivity of the
firm. Estimates of productivity from a recent paper by Clark and
Robert Feenstra are presented in Table 2.[9] The striking fact they
document is that low per capita income mainly reflects low productivity, both in 1910 and in 1990. In other words, it was not the
absence of capital, labour or technology which caused (and cause)
underdevelopment; but rather the inability to make the most of
them once they are in place.

The consulting firm McKinsey and Co. has produced studies of
productivity differences across countries, with similar results. For
example, two recent McKinsey studies found that moving an enterprise from the United States to Russia or Korea substantially reduces its productivity. What is one to make of this fact? McKinsey
argues that problems in the legal environment, protectionist poli-

---

9   Gregory Clark and Robert Feenstra, 'Technology in the Great Divergence', Work-
     ing Paper, University of California, Davis, May 2001.

cies, poor corporate governance and other institutional factors either undermine the ability to produce efficiently or weaken competitive pressures that otherwise would encourage efficiency. Other microeconomic research on Korean productivity by Anne Krueger and Jungho Yoo similarly shows that Korean conglomerates are value-destroying enterprises, which the authors attribute to poor corporate governance institutions (that is, rent-seeking, corruption and crony capitalism).[10]

A similar institutionalist perspective is found in Hernando DeSoto's influential and innovative work on the way in which corruption and ineffective vesting and enforcing of property rights destroy value. His first book, *The Other Path* (Harper & Row, New York, 1989), documents the high transaction costs of trying to organise and operate a small business in Peru, where seemingly endless hurdles await the brave entrepreneur (bureaucratic hurdles, of course, translate into endless opportunities for bribery). His second book, *The Mystery of Capital* (Basic Books, New York, 2000), generalises the argument by examining the vesting and enforcing of property rights in several countries. His central point is that good legal institutions of ownership have not evolved in most countries, and that this shortcoming produces endless opportunities for waste, extortion and corruption. Consequently, what Hayek called 'coercion' dominates economic transactions in developing economies. Wealth creation suffers.

The Heritage Foundation and the *Wall Street Journal* have constructed an index of freedom that quantifies the extent to which

---

10 'Chaebol Capitalism and the Currency-Financial Crisis in Korea', Working Paper, National Bureau of Economic Research, 2001. See also Sung Wook Joh, 'Korean Corporate Governance and Firm Performance', Working Paper, Korea Development Institute, July 2001.

Table 3 **Indices of institutional performance, selected countries**

	Rule of law	Corruption	Judicial efficiency	Economic freedom
	(Best score=10)	(Best score=10)	(Best score=10)	(Best score=1)
USA	10.0	8.6	10.0	1.75
Great Britain	8.6	9.1	10.0	1.80
Argentina	5.4	6.0	6.0	2.25
Japan	9.0	8.5	10.0	2.05
Thailand	6.3	5.2	3.3	2.20
Korea	5.4	5.3	6.0	2.25
Indonesia	4.0	2.2	2.5	3.55
Zimbabwe	3.7	5.4	3.7	4.25

Sources: The scores in the first three columns are on a scale of 1–10, where higher numbers indicate better performance. The scores in the last column are on a scale of 1–5, where lower numbers indicate better performance. Rule of law scores are from International Country Risk, and represent the average monthly score for the months of April and October from 1982 to 1995. Corruption scores are from the same source and are measured for the same dates. Judicial efficiency scores are from Business International Corporation and are averages for the period 1980–1983. Other countries' data for these three series can be found in David O. Beim and Charles W. Calomiris, *Emerging Financial Markets*, McGraw-Hill, 2001, pp. 184–5. The Index of Economic Freedom is the score for the year 2001. It measures the extent of economic freedom by weighting a variety of factors, including international trade, government intervention, monetary policy, foreign investment, banking and finance, wages and prices, property rights, regulation, and black markets. It is available on the Heritage Foundation website, http://database.townhall.com/heritage/index/indexoffreedom.cfm.

economic agents are free in different countries. Transparency International, International Country Risk and Business International Corporation also provide measures of the relative efficiency of judicial systems, the presence of rule of law, and the level of corruption. Table 3 reports measures of these indicators for the same countries included in Table 2. A comparison of these two tables shows that differences in economic efficiency are closely correlated with differences in the quality of the legal and political environment. Which way does the causation run? History is helpful here. While it is certainly logically possible to argue that good institutions are merely a luxury chosen by the wealthy, history shows that, in fact, good institutions preceded and made possible economic development.

To what extent has globalisation been associated with economic development and institutional reform? Our review of history from the medieval period up until the early nineteenth century showed that reaching outward was essential to the process of initial European economic development. Similarly, numerous econometric studies of the relationship between late nineteenth- and early twentieth-century globalisation of markets by Kevin O'Rourke, Jeffrey Williamson and others find important effects on economic growth from participating in global markets for commodities, labour and capital. O'Rourke and Williamson emphasise that during the pre-World War I period, emigration was the most powerful force for increasing growth worldwide, as it allowed workers to move from low-wage to high-wage countries. Lance Davis, Robert Cull and Robert Gallman, among others, emphasise the important role that capital flows played at crucial junctures in the growth experiences of the emerging market economies of that era.[11]

In the postwar era, limits on immigration into high-wage areas

---

11 See Jeffrey G. Williamson, 'Globalisation, Convergence and History', *Journal of Economic History*, 56, June 1996, pp. 1–30; Kevin O'Rourke and Jeffrey G. Williamson, *Globalisation and History*, MIT Press, Cambridge, MA, 1999; Lance E. Davis and Robert J. Cull, *International Capital Markets and American Economic Growth, 1820–1914*, Cambridge University Press, Cambridge, 1994; Lance E. Davis and Robert E. Gallman, *Evolving Financial Markets and International Capital Flows*, Cambridge University Press, Cambridge, 2001; and references contained in these works.

have meant that trade and capital flows, rather than emigration, are the dominant means through which globalisation produces economic growth. Jeffrey Sachs and Andrew Warner show that growth and trade liberalisation have been closely associated in the postwar era of globalised trade and capital flows.[12]

What about the distribution of income? To what extent does increased growth from globalisation translate into reductions in poverty? In their recent historical study of the effects of pre-World War I globalisation on income distribution, Peter Lindert and Jeffrey Williamson distinguish between changes in distributions of income within and between countries.[13] They find that participation in global markets in the pre-World War I era narrowed cross-country differences in income, and had little effect on within-country income distribution, implying substantial improvements in the lot of the poor living in countries that participated in global markets. Interestingly, in the pre-World War I era, income inequality worldwide increased, suggesting to casual observers that globalisation had produced rising inequality. In fact, the opposite is true; rising inequality across nations reflected the fact that countries participating in globalisation enjoyed substantial gains, while other countries saw their relative and absolute positions deteriorate.

In a forthcoming book on globalisation in the last twenty years, David Dollar of the World Bank has similarly found that participation in global trade significantly narrows income inequality across countries. He also shows that increases in trade

---

12 'Economic Reform and the Process of Global Integration', *Brookings Papers on Economic Activity*, I, 1995.

13 'Does Globalisation make the world more unequal?', Working Paper No. 8228, National Bureau of Economic Research, 2001.

and growth, and reductions in inequality and poverty, are all closely related to policies that promote free trade and the rule of law. These conclusions are visible in Figures 1–7, taken from Dollar's *World Bank Policy Research Report on Globalisation*. Figure 1 shows that the mean log deviation in household income has declined over the past two decades, and that this decline is entirely due to shrinking income inequality across countries. Figures 2–6 consider the extent to which convergence, or catching up, has occurred across countries since 1975. Figures 2, 5 and 6 indicate that catching up has been substantial, but has been confined largely to relatively open economies (a restatement of the Sachs-Warner result). Figure 3 shows that catching up has also been substantial for countries that enjoy high ratings for the presence of rule of law. Figure 4 presents Dollar's estimates of the effects of a one-standard-deviation improvement in the rule-of-law score (that is, the difference between Bolivia and Chile) on participation in the global economy; better rule of law is associated with increased foreign trade, higher foreign direct investment, and reduced reliance on worker remittances. Figure 7 explores the question of whether higher growth tends to benefit the poorest quintile of the population. Dollar finds that the growth rate in per capita income for the poorest segment of society matches the average growth rate for society as a whole. Growth is a powerful means for fighting poverty.

There is a growing body of new academic studies that confirm Dollar's findings. For example, Shangjin Wei and Yi Wu study the effect of globalisation on income inequality in China.[14] They find that the gap between relatively high urban and low rural income in

14 'Globalisation and Inequality: Evidence from within China', Working Paper, National Bureau of Economic Research, 2001.

Figure 1 **Worldwide household inequality, 1960–1999**

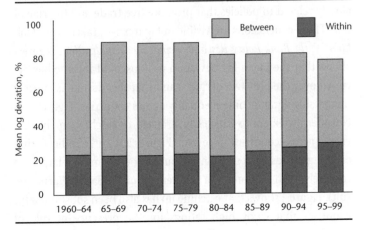

Figure 2 **Convergence among open economies, 1975–1999**

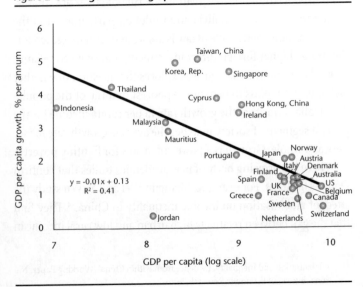

Figure 3 **Convergence among countries with good rule of law, 1975–1999**

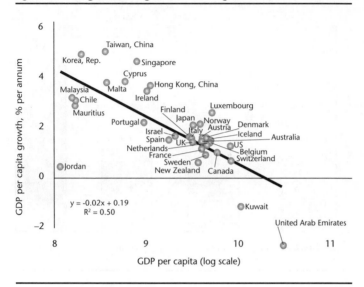

Figure 4 **Better rule of law leads to ...**

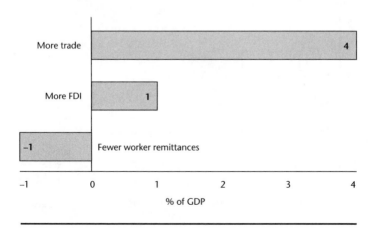

Figure 5 **Per capita GDP growth rates: post-1980 globalisers, %**

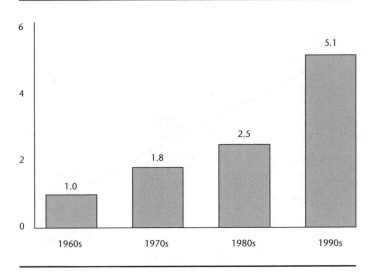

Figure 6 **Per capita GDP growth rates: non-globalisers, %**

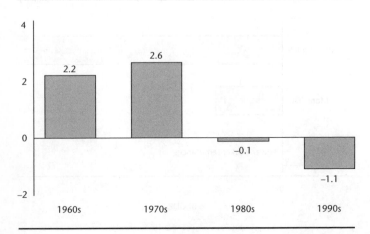

Figure 7 **Growth is good for the poor**

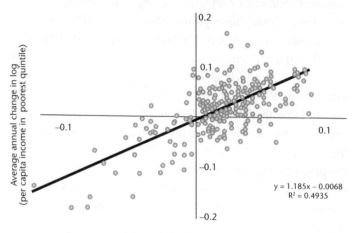

Average annual change in log (per capita income)

different regions of China has narrowed more in areas that were able to participate more in global trade.

What is the relative importance of the specific channels through which globalisation promotes improvements in productivity and institutions? It is hard to attach weights to the various influences, but a variety of channels seem to be important.

Competition in trade has not only permitted static efficiency gains, it has also encouraged technology transfer, which sometimes takes the form of foreign entry. In turn, foreign direct investment reduces the extent to which domestic production depends on existing domestic institutions, which can help to undermine practices of corruption and rent-seeking.

Second, flows of factors in and out of a country can be useful for allowing people and capital to move to countries where institutions work better. At a minimum, doing so frees some factors of production from home-grown inefficiency. O'Rourke and Williamson, and Lindert and Williamson, argue that, in the pre-World War I era, emigration was probably the single largest means through which globalisation improved the lot of the world's poor. While limits on emigration make it relatively less important today than in the past, there are still some important examples. Argentina has a population of some 36 million. The fact that over 3 million Argentines, typically among the best-educated and most productive workers, now reside in the United States, and the potential for more to follow, both mitigates the costs of Argentine economic failure today, and (one hopes) energises would-be reformers to find ways to stem the brain drain.

Third, while it is hard to quantify, the inflow of ideas about law and politics that has accompanied global commerce has probably played an important role, too. Long before the Soviet Union fell, its people were aware of, and desirous of being permitted to imitate, Western lifestyles. Before the 1989 Tiananmen Square massacre, heroic Chinese protesters frequently connected their efforts to the ideas of Enlightenment philosophers and statesmen from Europe and America. Despite the Chinese government's efforts to repress those ideas, including a recent crackdown on Chinese newspapers, these dictators are no match for the Internet – the voice of freedom is only a keystroke away.

Fourth, as these first three channels take effect, political and legal institutions change for the better as the result of incentives faced by corrupt leaders to share political power and reform the economic and legal system. The power-sharing brought by competitive European city building, empire building and industrialisation has a counterpart today in crony capitalist regimes. Liberalisation, privatisation and deregulation in emerging market countries are driven by greed, often the greed of politicians who see these as necessary to preserve their wealth in an increasingly competitive global economy. This process is one of virtuous 'co-ordination failure' among oppressive governments; if these rulers could have conspired to avoid reform they would have preferred to have done so. The new competitive world, after all, is requiring them to reduce taxes and share power with domestic entrepreneurs and foreign capitalists, and to commit to reining in their own authority by establishing predictable rules that will attract foreign entrants and allow domestic productivity to increase.

A recent study of financial-sector development over the past century by Raghuram Rajan and Luigi Zingales finds that international openness tends to constrain the wasteful rent-seeking activities of domestic banks and other firms that would otherwise retard financial and economic development.[15]

There are many current cases which illustrate that point. The recent reform of the Mexican banking system was a direct consequence of Mexico's outward orientation. Mexico decided to permit foreign entry into its financial system, and to force its domestic banks to modernise and compete as bona fide financial institutions as a means of improving economic performance after the collapse of its domestic banks in 1995. Now virtually the entire Mexican banking system is foreign-owned; foreign entry has fundamentally changed the role of banks in the economy and in the

---

15 'The Great Reversals: The Politics of Financial Development in the 20th Century', Working Paper No. 8178, National Bureau of Economic Research, March 2001.

political process, and has vastly improved the efficiency of the banking system.

Mexican banks used to be vehicles for managing political deals between their owners (who also owned large industrial conglomerates that borrowed from the banks) and politicians. Banks received government protection, from which they and their affiliated companies gained enormously; in exchange they provided various forms of assistance to politicians. Foreign entry undermined that unhealthy partnership, and replaced it with a modern banking system where banks are forced to compete, bear the gains and the losses from the decisions they make, and are thus encouraged to search out the most profitable, value-creating uses of their funds. Recent research by Ed Kane, and by Asli Demirguc-Kunt and Ross Levine, shows that foreign bank entrants have played this important role in many other countries recently, as well.[16]

To summarise, both in the distant past and in the recent past, global openness has spurred growth and alleviated poverty. Openness produces economic progress through direct channels (flows of commodities, information and factors of production), and via indirect channels, by improving institutions on which economic progress depends; openness reduces the economic power of domestic rent-seekers, and the competition among countries produced by an international wave of globalisation encourages rulers to liberalise.

---

16 Edward Kane, 'Capital Movements, Asset Values, and Banking Policy in Globalized Markets', Working Paper No. 6633, National Bureau of Economic Research, 1998; and Asli Demirguc-Kunt and Ross Levine, 'Opening to Foreign Banks: Stability, Efficiency, and Growth', Working Paper, World Bank, 1998.

Policy implications

I turn now to a discussion of policy implications, first for national economic policy, and second for the policies of international financial institutions (IFIs) – the IMF, World Bank and regional development banks.

The main implication for national economic policy for developing countries is that they should open themselves to global competition in trade, to foreign entry by firms, and to international capital flows. Some historians who are acquainted with the facts I have reviewed are more circumspect. Is it not true, after all, that many of the most successful industrialisers historically (including the United States) relied upon protective tariffs and non-tariff barriers to trade during critical early phases of their industrialisation? Yes, it is, but that does not imply that such a strategy is appropriate for developing economies today.

Japan's first wave of industrialisation was achieved without tariff protection, so tariff protection is certainly not a necessary condition for successful industrial catching up. One must also bear in mind that tariffs are equivalent to a tax on exports (according to the well-known Lerner Symmetry Theorem), and export taxation undermines the most viable means of rapid growth in developing economies today.

Moreover, in today's high-tech world, the most promising initial vehicle for industrialisation is often foreign direct investment by cutting-edge global producers. They do not need tariff protection since the technology they need is already developed, and low labour costs are enough of an enticement for entry. Import protection to coddle 'infant industries' during an initial phase of 'learning by doing' may have made some sense under British or American institutional conditions, but in today's developing economies it inevitably ends up producing rent-seeking, value-destroying firms that grow in political power rather than technical ability. For the purpose of stimulating industrialisation, effective government investment in basic education is a better use of limited government resources than subsidising import substitution.

In June this year I was in Beijing and had the opportunity to tour the PC manufacturing factory of Legend. Legend's experience nicely illustrates why the absence of protection can be a spur to efficient growth of infant industries, especially when those industries are able to import necessary knowhow and high-tech components. In 1984, Legend was established. It had an unexceptional growth experience for the first several years of its existence. In 1992, China substantially lowered its protective tariffs for computer manufacturers. Many inefficient Chinese manufacturers were unable to compete in the new unprotected environment. But one local manufacturer – Legend – was spurred forward by the need to compete. In response to foreign competition, in 1994 Legend developed a new business strategy based on, first, reducing costs – by focusing on its core business and shedding its distribution channels, and by importing components from abroad – and second, pursuing its comparative advantage by providing novel, customised PC products that targeted the special needs of Chinese computer purchasers. Legend's imported components are often designed in co-ordination with foreign producers, who have certain technological advantages but lack Legend's ability to gauge the needs of Asian purchasers. Legend also maintains research-and-development offices outside China, to help it develop its internal technological capability, which over time may reduce its dependence on foreign component producers. Legend now ranks eighth in the world in terms of PC sales. Clearly, this is a case in which the removal of tariff protection was a key ingredient in the development of efficient local industry.

A second policy implication is that the gains from global linkage, *per se*, are not guaranteed; gains depend on complementary changes in policy – specifically, reforming domestic institutions so that they are consistent with a competitive economy. But that linkage does not imply that reform must precede globalisation. Indeed, globalisation is the surest path to institutional reform.

Which reforms are most important, and what process should reform take? Institutional reform is never easy. At a minimum, it should ensure predictability and impartiality in administering the courts, effective legal protection of property and enforcement of contracts, transparent accounting, an effective commercial code, the absence of corruption and special favouritism towards some businesses by government subsidies, and a commitment to avoiding inflationary surges in budget deficits.

Effective financial institutions have also been key to the efficient allocation of capital and effort in every one of the major historical success stories. The British and the Dutch were the premier financial architects of the seventeenth century, creating joint stock companies, banks, central banks, and establishing the legal principles that permitted the use of negotiable instruments. They were also managing their public finances in innovative, effective ways by the end of the seventeenth century. America followed suit in the late eighteenth century with the establishment of a national monetary, financial and fiscal system, organised under the brilliant leadership of Alexander Hamilton. Germany's universal banking system of the late nineteenth century mobilised vast capital resources and channelled them with unprecedented speed and efficiency into the new products of the second industrial revolution, managing to underwrite and place industrial firms' equity offerings at unprecedented low costs. And Japan was also early to adopt sound currency and banking practices; by the end of the seventeenth century it had developed a credit system that was comparable to that of most of Europe, and later Japan was quite successful in imitating the best Western banking and central banking institutions of the late nineteenth century, which helped to lay the foundation of successful economic development.[17] Recent empirical studies of the growth-finance nexus indicate that effective financial institutions continue to exert a powerful influence on economic development.[18]

Although there are many useful success stories to learn from in all these areas of institution building, wholesale adoption of other countries' successful institutions is never as easy in practice as it sounds in theory. Even simple principles of property rights are harder to get right than one might imagine. For example, in *The Mystery of Capital*, DeSoto's discussion of the evolution of laws governing squatters' rights in the United States nicely illustrates how property law has to co-evolve with the specific historical circumstances of ownership and use; he persuasively argues that it is crucial to establish a process through which this can happen effectively. Institution building takes time, results from trial and error, and is specific to each country. DeSoto, like Hume and Hayek before him, recognises that good institutions cannot be fully reasoned out in advance from Cartesian introspection.

17 See Charles W. Calomiris, 'Banks and Banking', Working Paper, Columbia University, June 2001; and Peter Rousseau and Richard Sylla, 'Financial Systems, Economic Growth, and Globalisation', Working Paper, New York University, May 2001.

18 See David O. Beim and Charles W. Calomiris, *Emerging Financial Markets*, McGraw-Hill, New York, 2001, Chapters 2–5.

One of the elements that complicate institution building in the current political environment – particularly in the realm of banking and corporate governance – is the existence of contingent, implicit government protection of banks and other firms, which entails unhealthy risk sharing between the private sector and the government. Success in establishing good explicit legal rules and regulations and effective legal enforcement mechanisms is no longer enough to guarantee a good institutional environment. Recent experience – especially the expansion of the government safety net for banks and large industrial firms – has added new risks from incompetence or imprudence on the part of financial institutions, and has made effective fiscal reform much more difficult than it used to be. The presence of implicit protection via government bail-outs, especially of insolvent banks, means that taxpayers in developing countries are perpetually at risk of transferring vast sums of money to the privileged élites within their countries as the result of emergency transfers to insolvent banks and borrowers. Those contingent liabilities represent huge hidden subsidies, and result in frequent fiscal catastrophes. They also undermine competition and market discipline, and thus permit inefficient, value-destroying firms to absorb resources and further expand their political influence and favoured status.

Historically, market-disciplined banking systems responded to losses by curtailing asset risk, cutting dividends and raising new capital, all of which reassured bank debt-holders that the bank's problems would not translate into a significant increase in the likelihood of default on bank debt. Historically, banks that failed to maintain low risk of default faced the discipline of the market in the form of high interest costs and deposit withdrawals.

Government protection of banks the world over has undermined market discipline. Protected depositors have little incentive to worry about bank default, and thus banks have little incentive to manage risk prudently. Indeed, banks that are hardest hit by macroeconomic shocks now face strong incentives to *increase* risk in response to losses, since doing so gives insolvent or nearly insolvent banks a small chance of recovering their lost capital. Of course, most of the time, that risk-loving, 'resurrection' strategy results in large further losses, paid for by taxpayers.

How did costly bank protection policies come into being? Misguided economic theory and bad financial-macroeconomic history are partly to blame, as these have provided rationalisations for costly bail-outs out of fears about the instability that might result from failing to rescue insolvent banks. Ironically, historically relatively laissez-faire banking systems were far more stable than the protected banking systems of today, primarily because such banks were not protected by government, and thus faced strong incentives to manage risk prudently.

In my forthcoming book on historical banking crises, I find that in the forty years prior to World War I there were no more than seven episodes of severe banking-sector insolvency worldwide (that is, no more than seven episodes in which the negative net worth of banks reached or exceeded 1 per cent of GDP).[19] In only two of those cases did the costs exceed 4 per cent of GDP, and neither of those cases (Argentina in 1890 and Australia in 1893) saw bank insolvencies greater than 10 per cent of GDP.

Only in the Argentine case did a widespread banking collapse coincide with a substantial depreciation of the currency (the phe-

---

19   Charles W. Calomiris, 'Victorian Perspectives on the Banking Crises of the 1980s and 1990s', Manuscript, Columbia University, June 2001.

nomenon of 'twin crises' which has become so familiar today). Argentina was the one country that had established explicit government guarantees on mortgages (*cedulas*). That guarantee encouraged banks to originate and sell risky mortgages in volume, and those mortgages, because of their government guarantee, could be sold by banks at high prices; in fact, they were traded like treasury securities in the London market. When the mortgages defaulted, the government's finances collapsed, producing an enormous currency devaluation.

In the current era, banking system collapse has become the rule rather than the exception, and the magnitude of loss to government now frequently exceeds 10 per cent of GDP. There have been over one hundred significant banking collapses (by the 1 per cent of GDP loss criterion) in the past 25 years. More than 20 of those collapses have resulted in bail-out costs to the government in excess of 10 per cent of GDP, and many have reached or exceeded 20 per cent of GDP (including the recent examples of Mexico in 1995, and Thailand, Indonesia and Korea in 1997).

The problem is that what is called bank privatisation is in fact often quasi-privatisation – profits are private, losses are public. And the social losses exceed the insolvency of banks. Protected banks themselves often protect inefficient producers which depend on them for credit and which also seek and receive government bail-outs. From this perspective, it is not surprising that East Asian growth petered out in the mid-1990s. As Alwyn Young was the first to recognise, productivity growth had been meagre even among the 'tiger' economies by the mid-1990s.[20] Indeed, the weak-

---

20 Alwyn Young, 'The Tyranny of Numbers: Confronting the Statistical Realities of the East Asian Growth Experience', *Quarterly Journal of Economics*, 100, 1995, pp. 641–80.

Table 4 **Investment and growth in Asia's fastest-growing economies**

	Per-capita GDP growth rate % per annum 1973–1999	*Fixed investment/GDP 1973–1997*
Singapore	5.4	0.38
Hong Kong	4.1	0.27
Taiwan	5.3	0.24
South Korea	6.1	0.31
Malaysia	4.1	0.32
Thailand	4.8	0.31
China	5.4	0.30

Source: Angus Maddison, *The World Economy: A Millennial Perspective*, OECD, 2001, p. 146.

ness and ultimate collapse of the Thai, Korean and Indonesian banking systems provide an important perspective on rapid East Asian growth in GDP, one that reiterates the message of Table 3, that the Asian 'miracle' occurred in spite of the relatively unproductive use of inputs. The massive mobilisation of savings to finance domestic investment, not productivity growth, was the key to East Asian expansion, as shown in Table 4. Diminishing returns set in by the mid-1990s, and declining productivity relative to the US, along with looming fiscal risks from government protection of insolvent banks, were the key factors in the collapse of Asia's dollar exchange rate pegs. As the Asian economies slowed, and as their exchange rates became unsustainable, insolvent banks adopted resurrection strategies for taking on new risks, often by betting on foreign exchange rates or on junk bond issues.

The history of the high-flying Asian investment house Peregrine Investments was a microcosm of the Asian financial crisis. Peregrine brokered and participated in many of the most catastrophic speculations of 1997. Its management practices were remarkably haphazard, its compensation system almost wilfully designed to encourage imprudent lending, and its risk measurement and management virtually non-existent. Those failings reflected the fact that markets exerted little discipline on Peregrine's customers (including corrupt Indonesian firms and insolvent Korean banks), who were more than willing to take outlandish risks, and were themselves too incompetent to be able to detect failings in their investment bank.

Reform efforts to prevent bail-outs in developing-country banking systems have been slow. It is particularly challenging to construct institutions and laws to prevent governments from doing things that they are not legally bound to do. The United States and Chile have both passed laws that contemplate and limit *ad hoc* bail-outs of banks in clever and credible ways, so it is possible to do so. But the will is lacking to limit bail-outs in most countries because powerful vested interests favour them.[21]

In my view, this is not an insurmountable problem, although it will take years and many more bail-outs in many more countries to correct it. The good news is that costly banking collapses have a way of changing rules for the better – witness the Chilean reforms of the mid-1980s, or the Mexican banking reforms of the late 1990s. The latter coincided with the demise of the PRI as a political monopoly, largely in reaction to Mexico's 20 per cent of GDP cost for bailing out the protected bankers and their borrowers. Suharto ruled Indonesia for decades, but within months of Indonesia's

---

21 The propensity to bail out banks cannot be attributed to legitimate economic motives for doing so. Not only do bail-outs lend support to inefficient, risk-loving banks, and not only are they fiscally disastrous, they also tend to aggravate, rather than mitigate, business cycle downturns and credit crunches. For a fuller discussion of the social costs of bail-outs, see David O. Beim and Charles W. Calomiris, *Emerging Financial Markets*, McGraw-Hill, New York, 2001, Chapter 7 and references therein.

financial collapse he fell (here the bail-out bill was over 50 per cent of GDP). It will probably take more than the 1997 crisis to transform the corrupt state of affairs in Indonesia, or to lead to real reform in banking and corporate governance in Korea and Thailand, but it cannot take too many more such crises to produce change. The reason is a simple matter of arithmetic: no country can afford to pay for repeated collapses that costly. So, left to their own devices, countries that pursue quasi-privatisation strategies will end up having to choose between something much closer to true privatisation or a return to state control. I'm betting that the benefits of global engagement will make them choose true privatisation.

When they do, for many developing countries that will mean choosing to import financial service providers. Figure 8 is drawn from the recent World Bank Policy Research Report, *Finance for Growth* (2001). As this figure shows, most of the world's existing domestic banking systems are tiny – roughly one-third of the 166 countries surveyed by the World Bank had total banking system assets of under $1 billion. That small size reflects the history of developing-country governments' taxation and control of the financial sector, as well as the small size of many countries' economies. As financial sectors liberalise, the role of foreign entrants should expand. Small, undiversified banks operating only in one small developing economy will not be able to provide the full range of financial services or the diversification of assets of global universal banks. When those foreign bank entrants arrive they will offer more than the immediate gains of their knowhow and abundant capital; they also will change the political economy of banking by reducing the role of banks as instruments of crony capitalism.

Of course, banking and corporate governance reform is only part of the necessary recipe for successful development. Effective

Figure 8 **National financial systems ranked by size**

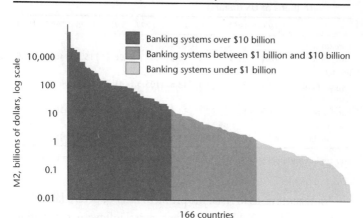

banking reforms can produce banking system stability only if they are combined with stable public finances. From 1991 to 1998, Argentina instituted some of the most creative and effective bank regulatory measures in the developing world, and won widespread respect for having credibly established market discipline in its banking system.[22] But beginning in 1996, government spending – financed by heavy sovereign borrowing abroad – began to undermine Argentine credibility. Three years of recession and almost certain financial collapse (despite repeated IMF efforts to postpone it) now threaten to bring the banking system and the currency board down alongside the collapse in the value of sovereign debt.

---

22 See Charles W. Calomiris and Andrew Powell, 'Can Emerging Market Bank Regulators Establish Credible Discipline? The Case of Argentina, 1992–1999', in F.S. Mishkin, *Prudential Supervision*, University of Chicago Press, Chicago, 2001.

Table 5 **Net private flows of capital to developing countries (billions of US dollars)**

	1990	1991	1992	1993	1994	1995	1996	1997	1998
Foreign direct investment	18.4	31.3	35.5	56.8	82.6	96.7	115.0	140.0	131.0
Portfolio investment	17.4	36.9	51.1	113.6	105.6	41.2	80.8	66.8	36.7
Bank loans and other	11.9	55.6	32.7	11.5	-35.5	55.4	16.3	-58.0	-104.0
Total net private flows	47.7	123.8	119.0	181.9	152.8	193.0	212.0	149.0	64.3

Source: International Monetary Fund, *International Capital Markets*, Table 1.3.1.

In Argentina, as in Asia, the problem has not been a lack of access to capital – as Table 5 shows, net capital inflows to developing economies have remained high and positive in every year of the past decade, despite repeated financial crises. Rather, the problem lies in the wasting of capital by imprudent governments, insolvent and inefficient banks, and crony capitalists.

In many countries, institutional shortcomings are even more basic than public- and private-sector financial failings. In most of Africa, and in many countries outside Africa, war, disease, famine and the absence of basic rule of law make it almost impossible to establish a viable economic system. Consider the depressing statistics of African decline reported in Table 6. Africa has been in economic freefall, in some countries for decades.

What, if anything, can the international financial institutions do to assist countries in building effective institutions, and which additional functions should be undertaken by the IFIs? Last year I served on the Meltzer Commission, a US Congressional Commission established to consider those questions. This is not the occasion to review and explain in detail all the recommendations of the

Table 6 **Per capita income collapse in the 13 largest sub-Saharan African countries**

	1998 population (000)	1998 per capita income as a percent of its previous peak	Peak year	Years since
Angola	10,865	36.6	1970	28
Cameroon	15,029	60.0	1986	12
Côte d'Ivoire	15,446	64.7	1980	18
Ethiopia	62,232	95.0	1983	15
Kenya	28,337	97.5	1990	8
Madagascar	14,463	55.4	1971	27
Mali	10,109	92.3	1979	19
Mozambique	18,641	63.3	1973	25
Nigeria	110,532	77.1	1977	21
Sudan	33,551	75.5	1977	21
Tanzania	30,609	88.8	1979	19
Zaïre	49,001	30.0	1974	24
Zimbabwe	11,004	100.0	1998	0
TOTAL	409,859	72.0	1980	18

Source: Angus Maddison, *The World Economy: A Millennial Perspective*, OECD, 2001, p. 165.

Commission.[23] But I would like to connect some of the reasoning in that report with the arguments in this paper.

The Meltzer Commission majority was very concerned that the IFIs had become part of the problem more often than part of the solution. The IFIs overestimate their ability to impose conditions on recalcitrant reformers, and thus their dollars are often wasted; as David Dollar and his colleagues at the World Bank showed in their monograph *Assessing Aid*, the success of assistance programmes depends crucially on the prior commitment to reform by the countries in question. Misspent assistance is worse

23 See Charles W. Calomiris, 'When Will Economics Guide IMF and World Bank Reform?', *Cato Journal*, 2000; and 'The IMF's Role as Imprudent Lender of Last Resort', *Cato Journal*, 1998.

than wasteful: aid is captured by corrupt rulers and distributed to their cronies as patronage. Development bank assistance encourages political jockeying, rent-seeking and wasteful allocation of public funds within recipient countries.

And the IFIs unwittingly increase financial risk, too. IMF lending to forestall financial crises sounds noble, but often is not; it facilitates counterproductive domestic government efforts to disguise and postpone the cost of dealing with insolvent financial institutions and their borrowers, or promotes unsustainable issuance of sovereign debt. IMF bail-outs also encourage reckless behaviour in other countries, in anticipation of future IMF support.

Not only do these IMF lending policies impose direct costs on taxpayers (by encouraging bail-outs and unsustainable fiscal policies); IMF loans, like those from the World Bank and the regional development banks, often help preserve the status quo by insulating domestic rent-seekers from the risk of loss or political disenfranchisement that would likely occur if rulers were forced to deal with the consequences of their corrupt or misguided policies. Argentina and Turkey today are the most obvious examples of countries that might benefit politically from the crucible of debt default.

There are, of course, bona fide, narrowly focused objectives, and potentially effective mechanisms for achieving them, which the IFIs might adopt. We on the Commission argued that alleviating poverty, offering intellectual and financial support for building core market institutions, co-ordinating global pollution control and enhancing market liquidity are legitimate objectives for the IFIs, which could be addressed much better than they currently are. But there is great opposition to what would be necessary to implement our proposed reforms – namely, narrowing the focus of the IFIs, constraining their behaviour, and improving their governance and accountability. That opposition is not just the result of intellectual disagreement. The IFIs serve a thinly veiled political purpose for the G7 countries, as a means of doling out favours to achieve *ad hoc* foreign policy objectives. Governments like slush funds.

Ultimately, however, I am optimistic about IFI reform. Just as I believe that many (though surely not all) developing-country governments will eventually be drawn to necessary institutional reform by the enormous costs of failing to reform, I am hopeful that the G7 governments will come to the conclusion that the problems of global poverty, disease and financial instability are too important to ignore.

And I think the multilateral agencies will be nudged in that direction by global progress itself, which will make it increasingly difficult for the G7 to use the IFIs as instruments of ad hoc foreign policy. A decade from now the global economy will be much more polycentric. Many emerging market countries – including China, Korea, Thailand, Argentina, Brazil, Mexico, Poland, Hungary and the Czech Republic, to name a few – will soon become fully fledged industrial nations. Multilateral agencies focused on bona fide economic objectives, with a more regionally decentralised administrative structure, will fit the global economy of the future better than the current structure, which is rooted in and subservient to the broad goals of the G7.

Still, the most important contribution the G7 can make to development is not IMF or World Bank reform, but rather a willingness to allow developing countries to compete in global markets, and a willingness to keep the doors open to immigrants. Perhaps the most important thing we can do to reduce poverty in Africa today is to cut tariffs on agricultural products, textiles and other

African exports. Recent research estimates that the economic gains to Africa from tariff reduction by the G7 would far exceed the total amount of aid provided to Africa by the G7 or the IFIs.[24]

As President Bush recently commented:

> Open trade is not just an economic opportunity [for the US], it is a moral imperative ... When we negotiate for open markets, we are providing new hope for the world's poor. And when we promote open trade, we are promoting political freedom. Societies that open to commerce across their borders will open to democracy within their borders, not always immediately, and not always smoothly, but in good time ... We must understand that the transition costs of open trade are dwarfed by open trade's benefits, that are measured not only in dollars and cents, but in human freedom, human dignity, human rights and human progress.

Yet the same President Bush who spoke so eloquently about the promise of global competition in May threatened steel import curbs in June in response to protectionist pressure from the US steel industry and its workers. Anti-globalist special interests, along with David Henderson's 'millennium collectivists', are a constant threat to global freedom. Logic and evidence gleaned from a thousand years of human progress may not be enough to defeat the anti-globalist naysayers. But we must try.

We should be encouraged in that effort by the successes of the past millennium in overcoming such resistance. We should also be encouraged by the widespread support that globalisation currently enjoys among the world's poorest inhabitants.

---

24 International Monetary Fund and World Bank Staff, *Market Access for Developing Countries' Exports*, 27 April 2001.

There has always been opposition to globalisation. In 1824, Lord Macaulay famously remarked that 'free trade, one of the greatest blessings which a government can confer on a people, is in almost every country unpopular'. O'Rourke and Williamson point out that opposition to globalisation was somewhat successful in reversing free trade prior to World War I, as the result of the same sort of political backlash that we are now facing.

Nevertheless, I am optimistic that globalisation will triumph, partly because of an important difference in the current debate – anti-globalisation today is not entirely a self-interested movement. The good intentions of many anti-globalisation protesters present advocates of globalisation with an opportunity. If well-intentioned protesters could be convinced that reversing globalisation would harm the world's poorest residents (as it surely would), some (perhaps many) of the protesters would change their minds about opposing globalisation.

Despite the attempts by NGOs and unions in the G7 countries, and crony capitalists and union workers in developing countries, to cast themselves as spokesmen for poor residents of developing economies, they do not, in fact, represent the interests or the viewpoint of the poor. Indeed, I believe it would be easy to show that there is widespread support for globalisation among the poor residents of developing economies. They understand better than anyone that the entry of foreign firms into their economies and the opening of export markets translate into more food on their tables and a chance for a better life for them and their children.

Proponents of globalisation need to find ways to make the voices of these stakeholders in globalisation heard among the din of the farcical demonstrations that now regularly accompany any significant gathering of international dignitaries. If that support could be mobilised and articulated, it would provide an important counterpoint to the self-interested and self-righteous anti-globalists, and possibly awaken some understanding among well-intentioned protesters of the human costs that would accompany an anti-globalist backlash.[25]

---

25 An example of such a contribution to the current debate is Thomas Friedman's book *The Lexus and the Olive Tree*, which contains many vignettes that illustrate in concrete terms the way globalisation produces opportunities for the poor in developing countries.

ABOUT THE IEA

The Institute is a research and educational charity (No. CC 235 351), limited by guarantee. Its mission is to improve understanding of the fundamental institutions of a free society with particular reference to the role of markets in solving economic and social problems.

The IEA achieves its mission by:

- a high-quality publishing programme
- conferences, seminars, lectures and other events
- outreach to school and college students
- brokering media introductions and appearances

The IEA, which was established in 1955 by the late Sir Antony Fisher, is an educational charity, not a political organisation. It is independent of any political party or group and does not carry on activities intended to affect support for any political party or candidate in any election or referendum, or at any other time. It is financed by sales of publications, conference fees and voluntary donations.

In addition to its main series of publications the IEA also publishes a quarterly journal, *Economic Affairs*, and has two specialist programmes – Environment and Technology, and Education.

The IEA is aided in its work by a distinguished international Academic Advisory Council and an eminent panel of Honorary Fellows. Together with other academics, they review prospective IEA publications, their comments being passed on anonymously to authors. All IEA papers are therefore subject to the same rigorous independent refereeing process as used by leading academic journals.

IEA publications enjoy widespread classroom use and course adoptions in schools and universities. They are also sold throughout the world and often translated/reprinted.

Since 1974 the IEA has helped to create a world-wide network of 100 similar institutions in over 70 countries. They are all independent but share the IEA's mission.

Views expressed in the IEA's publications are those of the authors, not those of the Institute (which has no corporate view), its Managing Trustees, Academic Advisory Council members or senior staff.

Members of the Institute's Academic Advisory Council, Honorary Fellows, Trustees and Staff are listed on the following page.

The Institute gratefully acknowledges financial support for its publications programme and other work from a generous benefaction by the late Alec and Beryl Warren.

ie a

The Institute of Economic Affairs
2 Lord North Street, Westminster, London SW1P 3LB
Tel: 020 7799 8900
Fax: 020 7799 2137
Email: iea@iea.org.uk
Internet: iea.org.uk

General Director	John Blundell

Editorial Director	Professor Colin Robinson

Managing Trustees

Chairman: Professor D R Myddelton

Robert Boyd
Michael Fisher
Malcolm McAlpine
Sir Michael Richardson
Professor Martin Ricketts

Lord Vinson, LVO
Sir Peter Walters
Linda Whetstone
Professor Geoffrey E Wood

Academic Advisory Council

Chairman: Professor Martin Ricketts

Graham Bannock
Professor Norman Barry
Professor Michael Beenstock
Professor Donald J Boudreaux
Professor John Burton
Professor Forrest Capie
Professor Steven N S Cheung
Professor Tim Congdon
Professor N F R Crafts
Professor David de Meza
Professor Richard A Epstein
Nigel Essex
John Flemming
Professor David Greenaway
Walter E Grinder
Professor Steve H Hanke
Professor Keith Hartley
Professor Peter M Jackson
Dr Jerry Jordan
Professor Daniel B Klein

Dr Anja Kluever
Professor David Laidler
Professor Stephen C Littlechild
Professor Antonio Martino
Dr Ingrid A Merikoski
Professor Patrick Minford
Professor David Parker
Professor Victoria Curzon Price
Professor Charles K Rowley
Professor Pascal Salin
Professor Pedro Schwartz
Professor J R Shackleton
Jane S Shaw
Professor W Stanley Siebert
Professor David Simpson
Professor Vernon L Smith
Professor Nicola Tynan
Professor Roland Vaubel
Professor Lawrence H White
Professor Walter E Williams

Honorary Fellows

Professor Armen A Alchian
Sir Samuel Brittan
Professor James M Buchanan
Professor Ronald H Coase
Dr R M Hartwell
Professor Terence W Hutchison
Professor Dennis S Lees

Professor Chiaki Nishiyama
Professor Sir Alan Peacock
Professor Ben Roberts
Professor Anna J Schwartz
Professor Gordon Tullock
Professor Sir Alan Walters
Professor Basil S Yamey

73

For information about subscriptions to IEA publications, please contact:

Subscriptions
The Institute of Economic Affairs
2 Lord North Street
London SW1P 3LB

Tel: 020 7799 8900
Fax: 020 7799 2137
Website: www.iea.org.uk/books/subscribe.htm

Other papers recently published by the IEA include:

WHO, What and Why?

Transnational Government, Legitimacy and the World Health Organization
Roger Scruton
Occasional Paper 113
ISBN 0 255 36487 3

The World Turned Rightside Up

A New Trading Agenda for the Age of Globalisation
John C. Hulsman
Occasional Paper 114
ISBN 0 255 36495 4

The Representation of Business in English Literature

Introduced and edited by Arthur Pollard
Readings 53
ISBN 0 255 36491 1

Anti-Liberalism 2000

The Rise of New Millennium Collectivism
David Henderson
Occasional Paper 115
ISBN 0 255 36497 0

Capitalism, Morality and Markets

Brian Griffiths, Robert A. Sirico, Norman Barry & Frank Field
Readings 54
ISBN 0 255 36496 2

A Conversation with Harris and Seldon

Ralph Harris & Arthur Seldon
Occasional Paper 116
ISBN 0 255 36498 9

Malaria and the DDT Story

Richard Tren & Roger Bate
Occasional Paper 117
ISBN 0 255 36499 7

A Plea to Economists Who Favour Liberty: Assist the Everyman

Daniel B. Klein
Occasional Paper 118
ISBN 0 255 36501 2

Waging the War of Ideas

John Blundell
Occasional Paper 119
ISBN 0 255 36500 4

The Changing Fortunes of Economic Liberalism

Yesterday, Today and Tomorrow
David Henderson
Occasional Paper 105 (new edition)
ISBN 0 255 36520 9

The Global Education Industry

Lessons from Private Education in Developing Countries
James Tooley
Hobart Paper 141 (new edition)
ISBN 0 255 36503 9

Saving Our Streams

The Role of the Anglers' Conservation Association in
Protecting English and Welsh Rivers
Roger Bate
Research Monograph 53
ISBN 0 255 36494 6

Better Off Out?

The Benefits or Costs of EU Membership
Brian Hindley & Martin Howe
Occasional Paper 99 (new edition)
ISBN 0 255 36502 0

Buckingham at 25

Freeing the Universities from State Control
Edited by James Tooley
Readings 55
ISBN 0 255 36512 8

Lectures on Regulatory and Competition Policy

Irwin M. Stelzer
Occasional Paper 120
ISBN 0 255 36511 X

Misguided Virtue

False Notions of Corporate Social Responsibility
David Henderson
Hobart Paper 142
ISBN 0 255 36510 1

HIV and Aids in Schools

The Political Economy of Pressure Groups and Miseducation
Barrie Craven, Pauline Dixon, Gordon Stewart & James Tooley
Occasional Paper 121
ISBN 0 255 36522 5

The Road to Serfdom

The Reader's Digest *condensed version*
Friedrich A. Hayek
Occasional Paper 122
ISBN 0 255 36530 6

Bastiat's *The Law*

Introduction by Norman Barry
Occasional Paper 123
ISBN 0 255 36509 8

To order copies of currently available IEA papers, or to enquire about availability, please contact:

Lavis Marketing
73 Lime Walk
Oxford OX3 7AD

Tel: 01865 767575
Fax: 01865 750079
Email: orders@lavismarketing.co.uk

Occasional Paper 124

A Globalist Manifesto for Public Policy

Charles Calomiris

ie

in association

NOMU

The worldwide trend towards privatisation, liberalisation and globalisation has produced substantial economic benefits. Nevertheless, liberalisation has had its shortcomings and there are potential threats to further progress, including in particular an anti-liberalisation backlash. Continuing progress depends on the ability to articulate a clear vision of the positive effects of global liberalisation and to establish institutions and policies which can help realise that vision. Reversing globalisation would harm the world's poorest inhabitants.

Professor Calomiris, well known for his work on national and international financial markets, examines the successes and failures of recent global liberalisation and derives a 'globalist manifesto' for public policy. His paper is a revised version of the tenth annual IEA Hayek Memorial Lecture given in July 2001.

The Institute of Economic Affairs
2 Lord North Street, Westminster
London SW1P 3LB
Tel: 020 7799 8900
Fax: 020 7799 2137
Email: iea@iea.org.uk
Internet: iea.org.uk

£7.50

ISBN 0 255 36525-X

9 780255 365253

Distributed by Lavis Marketing, Oxford